This book belongs to

The Backyard Bird

JOURNAL

A GUIDE TO
Recording and Observing
the Birds in Your Yard

ADAMS MEDIA
NEW YORK   LONDON   TORONTO   SYDNEY   NEW DELHI

Adams Media
An Imprint of Simon & Schuster, Inc.
100 Technology Center Drive
Stoughton, Massachusetts 02072

First Adams Media trade paperback edition January 2022

ADAMS MEDIA and colophon are trademarks of Simon & Schuster.

For information about special discounts for bulk purchases, please contact Simon & Schuster Special Sales at 1-866-506-1949 or business@simonandschuster.com.

The Simon & Schuster Speakers Bureau can bring authors to your live event. For more information or to book an event contact the Simon & Schuster Speakers Bureau at 1-866-248-3049 or visit our website at www.simonspeakers.com.

Interior design by Michelle Kelly
Illustrations by Sara Richard

Manufactured in the United States of America

1 2021

ISBN 978-1-5072-1805-1

Introduction

Backyard birding is an entertaining, engaging, and oftentimes surprising hobby that connects you with nature from the comfort of your own home. There is joy and care in creating a sanctuary for your local birds, providing their favorite foods, water sources, and shelters. It is gratifying to watch birds enjoy the haven you've created specifically for them.

Whether you are new to birding or have years of experience, you never lose the excitement of seeing a new bird in your yard. The first time you see its plumage, hear its song, and watch it in motion, you feel as if you've met a new friend. You can't wait for the next time it will return.

In *The Backyard Bird Journal*, you can record the details of all of the birds that visit your yard. In this easy-to-use logbook, you can note each species you spot, and include the date, time, and location of the sighting, along with the behaviors you see. There's also space to record additional sightings. Use your observations to make your backyard even more welcoming to the birds in your area.

Learn how many different species you can attract to your yard by referring to the Most Common Backyard Birds checklist at the end of this book. The list features fifty of the most commonly reported birds spotted in backyards of all types—from urban to suburban to rural settings—across the US.

Open the pages of this book to capture the fun, excitement, and wonder of nature found right in your backyard. Keep it handy in your favorite observation spot. Happy bird-watching!

BIRD: _____

	DATE & TIME	LOCATION
○ MALE ○ FEMALE		

VISITED A FEEDER? ○ YES ○ NO	STYLE OF FEEDER	FOOD IN FEEDER

VISITED A WATER SOURCE? ○ YES ○ NO	TYPE OF WATER SOURCE	

ACTIVITIES, BEHAVIORS, AND OTHER OBSERVATIONS

_____

_____

_____

_____

_____

_____

_____

_____

_____

_____

_____

_____

ADDITIONAL SIGHTINGS

DATE & TIME:

OBSERVATIONS:

DATE & TIME:

OBSERVATIONS:

DATE & TIME:

OBSERVATIONS:

DATE & TIME:

OBSERVATIONS:

DATE & TIME:

OBSERVATIONS:

BIRD:

	DATE & TIME	LOCATION
○ MALE ○ FEMALE		
VISITED A FEEDER? ○ YES ○ NO	STYLE OF FEEDER	FOOD IN FEEDER
VISITED A WATER SOURCE? ○ YES ○ NO	TYPE OF WATER SOURCE	

ACTIVITIES, BEHAVIORS, AND OTHER OBSERVATIONS

_____
_____
_____
_____
_____
_____
_____
_____
_____
_____
_____
_____
_____

ADDITIONAL SIGHTINGS

DATE & TIME:

OBSERVATIONS:

DATE & TIME:

OBSERVATIONS:

DATE & TIME:

OBSERVATIONS:

DATE & TIME:

OBSERVATIONS:

DATE & TIME:

OBSERVATIONS:

BIRD: _____

	DATE & TIME	LOCATION
○ MALE ○ FEMALE		

VISITED A FEEDER? ○ YES ○ NO	STYLE OF FEEDER	FOOD IN FEEDER

VISITED A WATER SOURCE? ○ YES ○ NO	TYPE OF WATER SOURCE	

ACTIVITIES, BEHAVIORS, AND OTHER OBSERVATIONS

_____

_____

_____

_____

_____

_____

_____

_____

_____

_____

_____

_____

_____

ADDITIONAL SIGHTINGS

DATE & TIME:

OBSERVATIONS:

DATE & TIME:

OBSERVATIONS:

DATE & TIME:

OBSERVATIONS:

DATE & TIME:

OBSERVATIONS:

DATE & TIME:

OBSERVATIONS:

BIRD: _____

	DATE & TIME	LOCATION
◯ MALE ◯ FEMALE		

	STYLE OF FEEDER	FOOD IN FEEDER
VISITED A FEEDER? ◯ YES ◯ NO		

	TYPE OF WATER SOURCE	
VISITED A WATER SOURCE? ◯ YES ◯ NO		

ACTIVITIES, BEHAVIORS, AND OTHER OBSERVATIONS

_____
_____
_____
_____
_____
_____
_____
_____
_____
_____
_____
_____
_____

ADDITIONAL SIGHTINGS

DATE & TIME:

OBSERVATIONS:

DATE & TIME:

OBSERVATIONS:

DATE & TIME:

OBSERVATIONS:

DATE & TIME:

OBSERVATIONS:

DATE & TIME:

OBSERVATIONS:

BIRD: _____

	DATE & TIME	LOCATION
○ MALE ○ FEMALE		

	STYLE OF FEEDER	FOOD IN FEEDER
VISITED A FEEDER? ○ YES ○ NO		

	TYPE OF WATER SOURCE
VISITED A WATER SOURCE? ○ YES ○ NO	

ACTIVITIES, BEHAVIORS, AND OTHER OBSERVATIONS

_____

_____

_____

_____

_____

_____

_____

_____

_____

_____

_____

_____

_____

ADDITIONAL SIGHTINGS

DATE & TIME:

OBSERVATIONS:

DATE & TIME:

OBSERVATIONS:

DATE & TIME:

OBSERVATIONS:

DATE & TIME:

OBSERVATIONS:

DATE & TIME:

OBSERVATIONS:

BIRD: _____

	DATE & TIME	LOCATION
○ MALE ○ FEMALE		

	STYLE OF FEEDER	FOOD IN FEEDER
VISITED A FEEDER? ○ YES ○ NO		

	TYPE OF WATER SOURCE	
VISITED A WATER SOURCE? ○ YES ○ NO		

ACTIVITIES, BEHAVIORS, AND OTHER OBSERVATIONS

_____

_____

_____

_____

_____

_____

_____

_____

_____

_____

_____

_____

_____

ADDITIONAL SIGHTINGS

DATE & TIME:

OBSERVATIONS:

DATE & TIME:

OBSERVATIONS:

DATE & TIME:

OBSERVATIONS:

DATE & TIME:

OBSERVATIONS:

DATE & TIME:

OBSERVATIONS:

BIRD: _____

	DATE & TIME	LOCATION
○ MALE ○ FEMALE		

	STYLE OF FEEDER	FOOD IN FEEDER
VISITED A FEEDER? ○ YES ○ NO		

	TYPE OF WATER SOURCE	
VISITED A WATER SOURCE? ○ YES ○ NO		

ACTIVITIES, BEHAVIORS, AND OTHER OBSERVATIONS

_____

_____

_____

_____

_____

_____

_____

_____

_____

_____

_____

_____

ADDITIONAL SIGHTINGS

DATE & TIME:

OBSERVATIONS:

DATE & TIME:

OBSERVATIONS:

DATE & TIME:

OBSERVATIONS:

DATE & TIME:

OBSERVATIONS:

DATE & TIME:

OBSERVATIONS:

BIRD: _____

	DATE & TIME	LOCATION
○ MALE ○ FEMALE		

	STYLE OF FEEDER	FOOD IN FEEDER
VISITED A FEEDER? ○ YES ○ NO		

	TYPE OF WATER SOURCE
VISITED A WATER SOURCE? ○ YES ○ NO	

ACTIVITIES, BEHAVIORS, AND OTHER OBSERVATIONS

_____

_____

_____

_____

_____

_____

_____

_____

_____

_____

_____

_____

ADDITIONAL SIGHTINGS

DATE & TIME:

OBSERVATIONS:

DATE & TIME:

OBSERVATIONS:

DATE & TIME:

OBSERVATIONS:

DATE & TIME:

OBSERVATIONS:

DATE & TIME:

OBSERVATIONS:

BIRD: _____

	DATE & TIME	LOCATION
○ MALE ○ FEMALE		

	STYLE OF FEEDER	FOOD IN FEEDER
VISITED A FEEDER? ○ YES ○ NO		

	TYPE OF WATER SOURCE	
VISITED A WATER SOURCE? ○ YES ○ NO		

ACTIVITIES, BEHAVIORS, AND OTHER OBSERVATIONS

_____

_____

_____

_____

_____

_____

_____

_____

_____

_____

_____

_____

_____

ADDITIONAL SIGHTINGS

DATE & TIME:

OBSERVATIONS:

DATE & TIME:

OBSERVATIONS:

DATE & TIME:

OBSERVATIONS:

DATE & TIME:

OBSERVATIONS:

DATE & TIME:

OBSERVATIONS:

BIRD: _____

	DATE & TIME	LOCATION
○ MALE ○ FEMALE		

VISITED A FEEDER? ○ YES ○ NO	STYLE OF FEEDER	FOOD IN FEEDER

VISITED A WATER SOURCE? ○ YES ○ NO	TYPE OF WATER SOURCE	

ACTIVITIES, BEHAVIORS, AND OTHER OBSERVATIONS

_____

_____

_____

_____

_____

_____

_____

_____

_____

_____

_____

_____

_____

ADDITIONAL SIGHTINGS

DATE & TIME:

OBSERVATIONS:

DATE & TIME:

OBSERVATIONS:

DATE & TIME:

OBSERVATIONS:

DATE & TIME:

OBSERVATIONS:

DATE & TIME:

OBSERVATIONS:

BIRD: _____

	DATE & TIME	LOCATION
○ MALE ○ FEMALE		

VISITED A FEEDER? ○ YES ○ NO	STYLE OF FEEDER	FOOD IN FEEDER

VISITED A WATER SOURCE? ○ YES ○ NO	TYPE OF WATER SOURCE	

ACTIVITIES, BEHAVIORS, AND OTHER OBSERVATIONS

_____
_____
_____
_____
_____
_____
_____
_____
_____
_____
_____
_____
_____

ADDITIONAL SIGHTINGS

DATE & TIME:

OBSERVATIONS:

DATE & TIME:

OBSERVATIONS:

DATE & TIME:

OBSERVATIONS:

DATE & TIME:

OBSERVATIONS:

DATE & TIME:

OBSERVATIONS:

BIRD: _____

	DATE & TIME	LOCATION
○ MALE ○ FEMALE		

	STYLE OF FEEDER	FOOD IN FEEDER
VISITED A FEEDER? ○ YES ○ NO		

	TYPE OF WATER SOURCE	
VISITED A WATER SOURCE? ○ YES ○ NO		

ACTIVITIES, BEHAVIORS, AND OTHER OBSERVATIONS

_____

_____

_____

_____

_____

_____

_____

_____

_____

_____

_____

ADDITIONAL SIGHTINGS

DATE & TIME:

OBSERVATIONS:

DATE & TIME:

OBSERVATIONS:

DATE & TIME:

OBSERVATIONS:

DATE & TIME:

OBSERVATIONS:

DATE & TIME:

OBSERVATIONS:

BIRD: _____

	DATE & TIME	LOCATION
○ MALE ○ FEMALE		

VISITED A FEEDER? ○ YES ○ NO	STYLE OF FEEDER	FOOD IN FEEDER

VISITED A WATER SOURCE? ○ YES ○ NO	TYPE OF WATER SOURCE	

ACTIVITIES, BEHAVIORS, AND OTHER OBSERVATIONS

_____

_____

_____

_____

_____

_____

_____

_____

_____

_____

_____

_____

_____

ADDITIONAL SIGHTINGS

DATE & TIME:

OBSERVATIONS:

DATE & TIME:

OBSERVATIONS:

DATE & TIME:

OBSERVATIONS:

DATE & TIME:

OBSERVATIONS:

DATE & TIME:

OBSERVATIONS:

BIRD: _____

	DATE & TIME	LOCATION
○ MALE ○ FEMALE		

VISITED A FEEDER? ○ YES ○ NO	STYLE OF FEEDER	FOOD IN FEEDER

VISITED A WATER SOURCE? ○ YES ○ NO	TYPE OF WATER SOURCE	

ACTIVITIES, BEHAVIORS, AND OTHER OBSERVATIONS

_____

_____

_____

_____

_____

_____

_____

_____

_____

_____

_____

ADDITIONAL SIGHTINGS

DATE & TIME:

OBSERVATIONS:

DATE & TIME:

OBSERVATIONS:

DATE & TIME:

OBSERVATIONS:

DATE & TIME:

OBSERVATIONS:

DATE & TIME:

OBSERVATIONS:

BIRD: _____

	DATE & TIME	LOCATION
○ MALE ○ FEMALE		

	STYLE OF FEEDER	FOOD IN FEEDER
VISITED A FEEDER? ○ YES ○ NO		

	TYPE OF WATER SOURCE	
VISITED A WATER SOURCE? ○ YES ○ NO		

ACTIVITIES, BEHAVIORS, AND OTHER OBSERVATIONS

_____

_____

_____

_____

_____

_____

_____

_____

_____

_____

_____

_____

_____

ADDITIONAL SIGHTINGS

DATE & TIME:

OBSERVATIONS:

DATE & TIME:

OBSERVATIONS:

DATE & TIME:

OBSERVATIONS:

DATE & TIME:

OBSERVATIONS:

DATE & TIME:

OBSERVATIONS:

BIRD: _____

○ MALE
○ FEMALE

DATE & TIME	LOCATION

	STYLE OF FEEDER	FOOD IN FEEDER
VISITED A FEEDER? ○ YES ○ NO		
VISITED A WATER SOURCE? ○ YES ○ NO	TYPE OF WATER SOURCE	

ACTIVITIES, BEHAVIORS, AND OTHER OBSERVATIONS

_____

_____

_____

_____

_____

_____

_____

_____

_____

_____

_____

_____

ADDITIONAL SIGHTINGS

DATE & TIME:

OBSERVATIONS:

DATE & TIME:

OBSERVATIONS:

DATE & TIME:

OBSERVATIONS:

DATE & TIME:

OBSERVATIONS:

DATE & TIME:

OBSERVATIONS:

BIRD: _____

	DATE & TIME	LOCATION
○ MALE ○ FEMALE		

	STYLE OF FEEDER	FOOD IN FEEDER
VISITED A FEEDER? ○ YES ○ NO		

	TYPE OF WATER SOURCE	
VISITED A WATER SOURCE? ○ YES ○ NO		

ACTIVITIES, BEHAVIORS, AND OTHER OBSERVATIONS

_____

_____

_____

_____

_____

_____

_____

_____

_____

_____

_____

_____

ADDITIONAL SIGHTINGS

DATE & TIME:

OBSERVATIONS:

DATE & TIME:

OBSERVATIONS:

DATE & TIME:

OBSERVATIONS:

DATE & TIME:

OBSERVATIONS:

DATE & TIME:

OBSERVATIONS:

BIRD: _____

	DATE & TIME	LOCATION
○ MALE ○ FEMALE		

	STYLE OF FEEDER	FOOD IN FEEDER
VISITED A FEEDER? ○ YES ○ NO		

	TYPE OF WATER SOURCE	
VISITED A WATER SOURCE? ○ YES ○ NO		

ACTIVITIES, BEHAVIORS, AND OTHER OBSERVATIONS

_____

_____

_____

_____

_____

_____

_____

_____

_____

_____

_____

ADDITIONAL SIGHTINGS

DATE & TIME:

OBSERVATIONS:

DATE & TIME:

OBSERVATIONS:

DATE & TIME:

OBSERVATIONS:

DATE & TIME:

OBSERVATIONS:

DATE & TIME:

OBSERVATIONS:

BIRD: _____

	DATE & TIME	LOCATION
○ MALE ○ FEMALE		

	STYLE OF FEEDER	FOOD IN FEEDER
VISITED A FEEDER? ○ YES ○ NO		

	TYPE OF WATER SOURCE	
VISITED A WATER SOURCE? ○ YES ○ NO		

ACTIVITIES, BEHAVIORS, AND OTHER OBSERVATIONS

_____

_____

_____

_____

_____

_____

_____

_____

_____

_____

_____

_____

ADDITIONAL SIGHTINGS

DATE & TIME:

OBSERVATIONS:

DATE & TIME:

OBSERVATIONS:

DATE & TIME:

OBSERVATIONS:

DATE & TIME:

OBSERVATIONS:

DATE & TIME:

OBSERVATIONS:

BIRD: _____

	DATE & TIME	LOCATION
◯ MALE ◯ FEMALE		
VISITED A FEEDER? ◯ YES ◯ NO	STYLE OF FEEDER	FOOD IN FEEDER
VISITED A WATER SOURCE? ◯ YES ◯ NO	TYPE OF WATER SOURCE	

ACTIVITIES, BEHAVIORS, AND OTHER OBSERVATIONS

_____

_____

_____

_____

_____

_____

_____

_____

_____

_____

_____

_____

_____

ADDITIONAL SIGHTINGS

DATE & TIME:

OBSERVATIONS:

DATE & TIME:

OBSERVATIONS:

DATE & TIME:

OBSERVATIONS:

DATE & TIME:

OBSERVATIONS:

DATE & TIME:

OBSERVATIONS:

BIRD: _____

	DATE & TIME	LOCATION
○ MALE ○ FEMALE		

	STYLE OF FEEDER	FOOD IN FEEDER
VISITED A FEEDER? ○ YES ○ NO		

	TYPE OF WATER SOURCE	
VISITED A WATER SOURCE? ○ YES ○ NO		

ACTIVITIES, BEHAVIORS, AND OTHER OBSERVATIONS

_____

_____

_____

_____

_____

_____

_____

_____

_____

_____

_____

_____

ADDITIONAL SIGHTINGS

DATE & TIME:

OBSERVATIONS:

DATE & TIME:

OBSERVATIONS:

DATE & TIME:

OBSERVATIONS:

DATE & TIME:

OBSERVATIONS:

DATE & TIME:

OBSERVATIONS:

BIRD: _____

	DATE & TIME	LOCATION
○ MALE ○ FEMALE		
VISITED A FEEDER? ○ YES ○ NO	**STYLE OF FEEDER**	**FOOD IN FEEDER**
VISITED A WATER SOURCE? ○ YES ○ NO	**TYPE OF WATER SOURCE**	

ACTIVITIES, BEHAVIORS, AND OTHER OBSERVATIONS

_____

_____

_____

_____

_____

_____

_____

_____

_____

_____

_____

_____

_____

ADDITIONAL SIGHTINGS

DATE & TIME:

OBSERVATIONS:

DATE & TIME:

OBSERVATIONS:

DATE & TIME:

OBSERVATIONS:

DATE & TIME:

OBSERVATIONS:

DATE & TIME:

OBSERVATIONS:

BIRD: _____

	DATE & TIME	LOCATION
◯ MALE ◯ FEMALE		
VISITED A FEEDER? ◯ YES ◯ NO	**STYLE OF FEEDER**	**FOOD IN FEEDER**
VISITED A WATER SOURCE? ◯ YES ◯ NO	**TYPE OF WATER SOURCE**	

ACTIVITIES, BEHAVIORS, AND OTHER OBSERVATIONS

_____
_____
_____
_____
_____
_____
_____
_____
_____
_____
_____
_____

ADDITIONAL SIGHTINGS

DATE & TIME:

OBSERVATIONS:

DATE & TIME:

OBSERVATIONS:

DATE & TIME:

OBSERVATIONS:

DATE & TIME:

OBSERVATIONS:

DATE & TIME:

OBSERVATIONS:

BIRD: _____

	DATE & TIME	LOCATION
○ MALE ○ FEMALE		
VISITED A FEEDER? ○ YES ○ NO	**STYLE OF FEEDER**	**FOOD IN FEEDER**
VISITED A WATER SOURCE? ○ YES ○ NO	**TYPE OF WATER SOURCE**	

ACTIVITIES, BEHAVIORS, AND OTHER OBSERVATIONS

_____

_____

_____

_____

_____

_____

_____

_____

_____

_____

_____

_____

ADDITIONAL SIGHTINGS

DATE & TIME:

OBSERVATIONS:

DATE & TIME:

OBSERVATIONS:

DATE & TIME:

OBSERVATIONS:

DATE & TIME:

OBSERVATIONS:

DATE & TIME:

OBSERVATIONS:

BIRD: _____

	DATE & TIME	LOCATION
○ MALE ○ FEMALE		

	STYLE OF FEEDER	FOOD IN FEEDER
VISITED A FEEDER? ○ YES ○ NO		

	TYPE OF WATER SOURCE	
VISITED A WATER SOURCE? ○ YES ○ NO		

ACTIVITIES, BEHAVIORS, AND OTHER OBSERVATIONS

_____

_____

_____

_____

_____

_____

_____

_____

_____

_____

_____

_____

ADDITIONAL SIGHTINGS

DATE & TIME:

OBSERVATIONS:

DATE & TIME:

OBSERVATIONS:

DATE & TIME:

OBSERVATIONS:

DATE & TIME:

OBSERVATIONS:

DATE & TIME:

OBSERVATIONS:

BIRD: _____

	DATE & TIME	LOCATION
○ MALE ○ FEMALE		

VISITED A FEEDER? ○ YES ○ NO	STYLE OF FEEDER	FOOD IN FEEDER

VISITED A WATER SOURCE? ○ YES ○ NO	TYPE OF WATER SOURCE	

ACTIVITIES, BEHAVIORS, AND OTHER OBSERVATIONS

_____
_____
_____
_____
_____
_____
_____
_____
_____
_____
_____
_____
_____
_____

ADDITIONAL SIGHTINGS

DATE & TIME:

OBSERVATIONS:

DATE & TIME:

OBSERVATIONS:

DATE & TIME:

OBSERVATIONS:

DATE & TIME:

OBSERVATIONS:

DATE & TIME:

OBSERVATIONS:

BIRD: _____

○ MALE
○ FEMALE

DATE & TIME	LOCATION

	STYLE OF FEEDER	FOOD IN FEEDER
VISITED A FEEDER? ○ YES ○ NO		

	TYPE OF WATER SOURCE
VISITED A WATER SOURCE? ○ YES ○ NO	

ACTIVITIES, BEHAVIORS, AND OTHER OBSERVATIONS

_____

_____

_____

_____

_____

_____

_____

_____

_____

_____

_____

_____

ADDITIONAL SIGHTINGS

DATE & TIME:

OBSERVATIONS:

DATE & TIME:

OBSERVATIONS:

DATE & TIME:

OBSERVATIONS:

DATE & TIME:

OBSERVATIONS:

DATE & TIME:

OBSERVATIONS:

BIRD: _____

	DATE & TIME	LOCATION
○ MALE ○ FEMALE		

	STYLE OF FEEDER	FOOD IN FEEDER
VISITED A FEEDER? ○ YES ○ NO		

	TYPE OF WATER SOURCE	
VISITED A WATER SOURCE? ○ YES ○ NO		

ACTIVITIES, BEHAVIORS, AND OTHER OBSERVATIONS

_____

_____

_____

_____

_____

_____

_____

_____

_____

_____

_____

_____

ADDITIONAL SIGHTINGS

DATE & TIME:

OBSERVATIONS:

DATE & TIME:

OBSERVATIONS:

DATE & TIME:

OBSERVATIONS:

DATE & TIME:

OBSERVATIONS:

DATE & TIME:

OBSERVATIONS:

BIRD: _____

	DATE & TIME	LOCATION
○ MALE ○ FEMALE		

	STYLE OF FEEDER	FOOD IN FEEDER
VISITED A FEEDER? ○ YES ○ NO		

	TYPE OF WATER SOURCE
VISITED A WATER SOURCE? ○ YES ○ NO	

ACTIVITIES, BEHAVIORS, AND OTHER OBSERVATIONS

_____
_____
_____
_____
_____
_____
_____
_____
_____
_____
_____
_____

ADDITIONAL SIGHTINGS

DATE & TIME:

OBSERVATIONS:

DATE & TIME:

OBSERVATIONS:

DATE & TIME:

OBSERVATIONS:

DATE & TIME:

OBSERVATIONS:

DATE & TIME:

OBSERVATIONS:

BIRD: _____

	DATE & TIME	LOCATION
○ MALE ○ FEMALE		

	STYLE OF FEEDER	FOOD IN FEEDER
VISITED A FEEDER? ○ YES ○ NO		

	TYPE OF WATER SOURCE	
VISITED A WATER SOURCE? ○ YES ○ NO		

ACTIVITIES, BEHAVIORS, AND OTHER OBSERVATIONS

_____

_____

_____

_____

_____

_____

_____

_____

_____

_____

_____

_____

ADDITIONAL SIGHTINGS

DATE & TIME:

OBSERVATIONS:

DATE & TIME:

OBSERVATIONS:

DATE & TIME:

OBSERVATIONS:

DATE & TIME:

OBSERVATIONS:

DATE & TIME:

OBSERVATIONS:

BIRD: _____

	DATE & TIME	LOCATION
○ MALE ○ FEMALE		

	STYLE OF FEEDER	FOOD IN FEEDER
VISITED A FEEDER? ○ YES ○ NO		

	TYPE OF WATER SOURCE	
VISITED A WATER SOURCE? ○ YES ○ NO		

ACTIVITIES, BEHAVIORS, AND OTHER OBSERVATIONS

_____

_____

_____

_____

_____

_____

_____

_____

_____

_____

_____

_____

ADDITIONAL SIGHTINGS

DATE & TIME:

OBSERVATIONS:

DATE & TIME:

OBSERVATIONS:

DATE & TIME:

OBSERVATIONS:

DATE & TIME:

OBSERVATIONS:

DATE & TIME:

OBSERVATIONS:

BIRD: _____

	DATE & TIME	LOCATION
○ MALE		
○ FEMALE		

	STYLE OF FEEDER	FOOD IN FEEDER
VISITED A FEEDER? ○ YES ○ NO		

	TYPE OF WATER SOURCE
VISITED A WATER SOURCE? ○ YES ○ NO	

ACTIVITIES, BEHAVIORS, AND OTHER OBSERVATIONS

_____

_____

_____

_____

_____

_____

_____

_____

_____

_____

_____

_____

ADDITIONAL SIGHTINGS

DATE & TIME:

OBSERVATIONS:

DATE & TIME:

OBSERVATIONS:

DATE & TIME:

OBSERVATIONS:

DATE & TIME:

OBSERVATIONS:

DATE & TIME:

OBSERVATIONS:

BIRD: _____

	DATE & TIME	LOCATION
○ MALE ○ FEMALE		

VISITED A FEEDER? ○ YES ○ NO	STYLE OF FEEDER	FOOD IN FEEDER

VISITED A WATER SOURCE? ○ YES ○ NO	TYPE OF WATER SOURCE

ACTIVITIES, BEHAVIORS, AND OTHER OBSERVATIONS

_____

_____

_____

_____

_____

_____

_____

_____

_____

_____

_____

_____

_____

ADDITIONAL SIGHTINGS

DATE & TIME:

OBSERVATIONS:

DATE & TIME:

OBSERVATIONS:

DATE & TIME:

OBSERVATIONS:

DATE & TIME:

OBSERVATIONS:

DATE & TIME:

OBSERVATIONS:

BIRD: _____

	DATE & TIME	LOCATION
○ MALE ○ FEMALE		

	STYLE OF FEEDER	FOOD IN FEEDER
VISITED A FEEDER? ○ YES ○ NO		

	TYPE OF WATER SOURCE	
VISITED A WATER SOURCE? ○ YES ○ NO		

ACTIVITIES, BEHAVIORS, AND OTHER OBSERVATIONS

_____
_____
_____
_____
_____
_____
_____
_____
_____
_____
_____
_____

ADDITIONAL SIGHTINGS

DATE & TIME:

OBSERVATIONS:

DATE & TIME:

OBSERVATIONS:

DATE & TIME:

OBSERVATIONS:

DATE & TIME:

OBSERVATIONS:

DATE & TIME:

OBSERVATIONS:

BIRD: _____

○ MALE
○ FEMALE

DATE & TIME	LOCATION

VISITED A FEEDER? ○ YES ○ NO	STYLE OF FEEDER	FOOD IN FEEDER

VISITED A WATER SOURCE? ○ YES ○ NO	TYPE OF WATER SOURCE

ACTIVITIES, BEHAVIORS, AND OTHER OBSERVATIONS

_____
_____
_____
_____
_____
_____
_____
_____
_____
_____
_____
_____
_____

ADDITIONAL SIGHTINGS

DATE & TIME:

OBSERVATIONS:

DATE & TIME:

OBSERVATIONS:

DATE & TIME:

OBSERVATIONS:

DATE & TIME:

OBSERVATIONS:

DATE & TIME:

OBSERVATIONS:

BIRD: _____

	DATE & TIME	LOCATION
○ MALE ○ FEMALE		
VISITED A FEEDER? ○ YES ○ NO	STYLE OF FEEDER	FOOD IN FEEDER
VISITED A WATER SOURCE? ○ YES ○ NO	TYPE OF WATER SOURCE	

ACTIVITIES, BEHAVIORS, AND OTHER OBSERVATIONS

_____

_____

_____

_____

_____

_____

_____

_____

_____

_____

_____

_____

ADDITIONAL SIGHTINGS

DATE & TIME:

OBSERVATIONS:

DATE & TIME:

OBSERVATIONS:

DATE & TIME:

OBSERVATIONS:

DATE & TIME:

OBSERVATIONS:

DATE & TIME:

OBSERVATIONS:

BIRD: _____

○ MALE
○ FEMALE

DATE & TIME	LOCATION

VISITED A FEEDER? ○ YES ○ NO	STYLE OF FEEDER	FOOD IN FEEDER

VISITED A WATER SOURCE? ○ YES ○ NO	TYPE OF WATER SOURCE	

ACTIVITIES, BEHAVIORS, AND OTHER OBSERVATIONS

_____

_____

_____

_____

_____

_____

_____

_____

_____

_____

_____

_____

ADDITIONAL SIGHTINGS

DATE & TIME:

OBSERVATIONS:

DATE & TIME:

OBSERVATIONS:

DATE & TIME:

OBSERVATIONS:

DATE & TIME:

OBSERVATIONS:

DATE & TIME:

OBSERVATIONS:

BIRD: _____

	DATE & TIME	LOCATION
O MALE O FEMALE		
VISITED A FEEDER? O YES O NO	STYLE OF FEEDER	FOOD IN FEEDER
VISITED A WATER SOURCE? O YES O NO	TYPE OF WATER SOURCE	

ACTIVITIES, BEHAVIORS, AND OTHER OBSERVATIONS

_____

_____

_____ .

_____

_____

_____

_____

_____

_____

_____

_____

_____

ADDITIONAL SIGHTINGS

DATE & TIME:

OBSERVATIONS:

DATE & TIME:

OBSERVATIONS:

DATE & TIME:

OBSERVATIONS:

DATE & TIME:

OBSERVATIONS:

DATE & TIME:

OBSERVATIONS:

BIRD: _____

○ MALE
○ FEMALE

DATE & TIME	LOCATION

VISITED A FEEDER? ○ YES ○ NO	STYLE OF FEEDER	FOOD IN FEEDER

VISITED A WATER SOURCE? ○ YES ○ NO	TYPE OF WATER SOURCE	

ACTIVITIES, BEHAVIORS, AND OTHER OBSERVATIONS

_____

_____

_____

_____

_____

_____

_____

_____

_____

_____

_____

_____

ADDITIONAL SIGHTINGS

DATE & TIME:

OBSERVATIONS:

DATE & TIME:

OBSERVATIONS:

DATE & TIME:

OBSERVATIONS:

DATE & TIME:

OBSERVATIONS:

DATE & TIME:

OBSERVATIONS:

BIRD: _____

○ MALE
○ FEMALE

DATE & TIME	LOCATION

VISITED A FEEDER? ○ YES ○ NO	STYLE OF FEEDER	FOOD IN FEEDER

VISITED A WATER SOURCE? ○ YES ○ NO	TYPE OF WATER SOURCE	

ACTIVITIES, BEHAVIORS, AND OTHER OBSERVATIONS

_____

_____

_____

_____

_____

_____

_____

_____

_____

_____

_____

_____

_____

ADDITIONAL SIGHTINGS

DATE & TIME:

OBSERVATIONS:

DATE & TIME:

OBSERVATIONS:

DATE & TIME:

OBSERVATIONS:

DATE & TIME:

OBSERVATIONS:

DATE & TIME:

OBSERVATIONS:

BIRD: _____

○ MALE
○ FEMALE

DATE & TIME	LOCATION

VISITED A FEEDER? ○ YES ○ NO	STYLE OF FEEDER	FOOD IN FEEDER

VISITED A WATER SOURCE? ○ YES ○ NO	TYPE OF WATER SOURCE	

ACTIVITIES, BEHAVIORS, AND OTHER OBSERVATIONS

_____
_____
_____
_____
_____
_____
_____
_____
_____
_____
_____
_____

ADDITIONAL SIGHTINGS

DATE & TIME:

OBSERVATIONS:

DATE & TIME:

OBSERVATIONS:

DATE & TIME:

OBSERVATIONS:

DATE & TIME:

OBSERVATIONS:

DATE & TIME:

OBSERVATIONS:

BIRD: _____

	DATE & TIME	LOCATION
○ MALE ○ FEMALE		

	STYLE OF FEEDER	FOOD IN FEEDER
VISITED A FEEDER? ○ YES ○ NO		

	TYPE OF WATER SOURCE	
VISITED A WATER SOURCE? ○ YES ○ NO		

ACTIVITIES, BEHAVIORS, AND OTHER OBSERVATIONS

_____

_____

_____

_____

_____

_____

_____

_____

_____

_____

_____

_____

ADDITIONAL SIGHTINGS

DATE & TIME:

OBSERVATIONS:

DATE & TIME:

OBSERVATIONS:

DATE & TIME:

OBSERVATIONS:

DATE & TIME:

OBSERVATIONS:

DATE & TIME:

OBSERVATIONS:

BIRD: _____

○ MALE
○ FEMALE

DATE & TIME	LOCATION

VISITED A FEEDER? ○ YES ○ NO	STYLE OF FEEDER	FOOD IN FEEDER

VISITED A WATER SOURCE? ○ YES ○ NO	TYPE OF WATER SOURCE	

ACTIVITIES, BEHAVIORS, AND OTHER OBSERVATIONS

_____

_____

_____

_____

_____

_____

_____

_____

_____

_____

_____

_____

ADDITIONAL SIGHTINGS

DATE & TIME:

OBSERVATIONS:

DATE & TIME:

OBSERVATIONS:

DATE & TIME:

OBSERVATIONS:

DATE & TIME:

OBSERVATIONS:

DATE & TIME:

OBSERVATIONS:

BIRD: _____

○ MALE
○ FEMALE

DATE & TIME	LOCATION

VISITED A FEEDER? ○ YES ○ NO	STYLE OF FEEDER	FOOD IN FEEDER

VISITED A WATER SOURCE? ○ YES ○ NO	TYPE OF WATER SOURCE

ACTIVITIES, BEHAVIORS, AND OTHER OBSERVATIONS

_____

_____

_____

_____

_____

_____

_____

_____

_____

_____

_____

_____

ADDITIONAL SIGHTINGS

DATE & TIME:

OBSERVATIONS:

DATE & TIME:

OBSERVATIONS:

DATE & TIME:

OBSERVATIONS:

DATE & TIME:

OBSERVATIONS:

DATE & TIME:

OBSERVATIONS:

BIRD: _____

	DATE & TIME	LOCATION
○ MALE ○ FEMALE		

	STYLE OF FEEDER	FOOD IN FEEDER
VISITED A FEEDER? ○ YES ○ NO		

	TYPE OF WATER SOURCE	
VISITED A WATER SOURCE? ○ YES ○ NO		

ACTIVITIES, BEHAVIORS, AND OTHER OBSERVATIONS

_____

_____

_____

_____

_____

_____

_____

_____

_____

_____

_____

_____

ADDITIONAL SIGHTINGS

DATE & TIME:

OBSERVATIONS:

DATE & TIME:

OBSERVATIONS:

DATE & TIME:

OBSERVATIONS:

DATE & TIME:

OBSERVATIONS:

DATE & TIME:

OBSERVATIONS:

BIRD: _____

	DATE & TIME	LOCATION
○ MALE ○ FEMALE		

	STYLE OF FEEDER	FOOD IN FEEDER
VISITED A FEEDER? ○ YES ○ NO		

	TYPE OF WATER SOURCE	
VISITED A WATER SOURCE? ○ YES ○ NO		

ACTIVITIES, BEHAVIORS, AND OTHER OBSERVATIONS

_____

_____

_____

_____

_____

_____

_____

_____

_____

_____

_____

_____

ADDITIONAL SIGHTINGS

DATE & TIME:

OBSERVATIONS:

DATE & TIME:

OBSERVATIONS:

DATE & TIME:

OBSERVATIONS:

DATE & TIME:

OBSERVATIONS:

DATE & TIME:

OBSERVATIONS:

BIRD: _____

	DATE & TIME	LOCATION
○ MALE ○ FEMALE		

	STYLE OF FEEDER	FOOD IN FEEDER
VISITED A FEEDER? ○ YES ○ NO		

	TYPE OF WATER SOURCE
VISITED A WATER SOURCE? ○ YES ○ NO	

ACTIVITIES, BEHAVIORS, AND OTHER OBSERVATIONS

_____

_____

_____

_____

_____

_____

_____

_____

_____

_____

_____

_____

_____

ADDITIONAL SIGHTINGS

DATE & TIME:

OBSERVATIONS:

DATE & TIME:

OBSERVATIONS:

DATE & TIME:

OBSERVATIONS:

DATE & TIME:

OBSERVATIONS:

DATE & TIME:

OBSERVATIONS:

BIRD: _____

	DATE & TIME	LOCATION
○ MALE ○ FEMALE		

	STYLE OF FEEDER	FOOD IN FEEDER
VISITED A FEEDER? ○ YES ○ NO		

	TYPE OF WATER SOURCE
VISITED A WATER SOURCE? ○ YES ○ NO	

ACTIVITIES, BEHAVIORS, AND OTHER OBSERVATIONS

_____

_____

_____

_____

_____

_____

_____

_____

_____

_____

_____

_____

_____

ADDITIONAL SIGHTINGS

DATE & TIME:

OBSERVATIONS:

DATE & TIME:

OBSERVATIONS:

DATE & TIME:

OBSERVATIONS:

DATE & TIME:

OBSERVATIONS:

DATE & TIME:

OBSERVATIONS:

BIRD: _____

	DATE & TIME	LOCATION
○ MALE ○ FEMALE		

	STYLE OF FEEDER	FOOD IN FEEDER
VISITED A FEEDER? ○ YES ○ NO		

	TYPE OF WATER SOURCE	
VISITED A WATER SOURCE? ○ YES ○ NO		

ACTIVITIES, BEHAVIORS, AND OTHER OBSERVATIONS

_____

_____

_____

_____

_____

_____

_____

_____

_____

_____

_____

_____

ADDITIONAL SIGHTINGS

DATE & TIME:

OBSERVATIONS:

DATE & TIME:

OBSERVATIONS:

DATE & TIME:

OBSERVATIONS:

DATE & TIME:

OBSERVATIONS:

DATE & TIME:

OBSERVATIONS:

BIRD: _____

○ MALE
○ FEMALE

DATE & TIME	LOCATION

VISITED A FEEDER?

○ YES
○ NO

STYLE OF FEEDER	FOOD IN FEEDER

VISITED A WATER SOURCE?

○ YES
○ NO

TYPE OF WATER SOURCE

ACTIVITIES, BEHAVIORS, AND OTHER OBSERVATIONS

_____

_____

_____

_____

_____

_____

_____

_____

_____

_____

_____

_____

_____

ADDITIONAL SIGHTINGS

DATE & TIME:

OBSERVATIONS:

DATE & TIME:

OBSERVATIONS:

DATE & TIME:

OBSERVATIONS:

DATE & TIME:

OBSERVATIONS:

DATE & TIME:

OBSERVATIONS:

BIRD: _____

○ MALE
○ FEMALE

DATE & TIME	LOCATION

	STYLE OF FEEDER	FOOD IN FEEDER
VISITED A FEEDER? ○ YES ○ NO		
VISITED A WATER SOURCE? ○ YES ○ NO	TYPE OF WATER SOURCE	

ACTIVITIES, BEHAVIORS, AND OTHER OBSERVATIONS

_____
_____
_____
_____
_____
_____
_____
_____
_____
_____
_____
_____
_____

ADDITIONAL SIGHTINGS

DATE & TIME:

OBSERVATIONS:

DATE & TIME:

OBSERVATIONS:

DATE & TIME:

OBSERVATIONS:

DATE & TIME:

OBSERVATIONS:

DATE & TIME:

OBSERVATIONS:

BIRD: _____

○ MALE
○ FEMALE

DATE & TIME	LOCATION

VISITED A FEEDER? ○ YES ○ NO	STYLE OF FEEDER	FOOD IN FEEDER

VISITED A WATER SOURCE? ○ YES ○ NO	TYPE OF WATER SOURCE

ACTIVITIES, BEHAVIORS, AND OTHER OBSERVATIONS

_____

_____

_____

_____

_____

_____

_____

_____

_____

_____

_____

_____

ADDITIONAL SIGHTINGS

DATE & TIME:

OBSERVATIONS:

DATE & TIME:

OBSERVATIONS:

DATE & TIME:

OBSERVATIONS:

DATE & TIME:

OBSERVATIONS:

DATE & TIME:

OBSERVATIONS:

BIRD: _____

○ MALE
○ FEMALE

DATE & TIME	LOCATION

VISITED A FEEDER? ○ YES ○ NO	STYLE OF FEEDER	FOOD IN FEEDER

VISITED A WATER SOURCE? ○ YES ○ NO	TYPE OF WATER SOURCE	

ACTIVITIES, BEHAVIORS, AND OTHER OBSERVATIONS

_____

_____

_____

_____

_____

_____

_____

_____

_____

_____

_____

_____

ADDITIONAL SIGHTINGS

DATE & TIME:

OBSERVATIONS:

DATE & TIME:

OBSERVATIONS:

DATE & TIME:

OBSERVATIONS:

DATE & TIME:

OBSERVATIONS:

DATE & TIME:

OBSERVATIONS:

BIRD: _____

○ MALE
○ FEMALE

DATE & TIME	LOCATION

VISITED A FEEDER? ○ YES ○ NO	STYLE OF FEEDER	FOOD IN FEEDER

VISITED A WATER SOURCE? ○ YES ○ NO	TYPE OF WATER SOURCE

ACTIVITIES, BEHAVIORS, AND OTHER OBSERVATIONS

_____

_____

_____

_____

_____

_____

_____

_____

_____

_____

_____

_____

_____

ADDITIONAL SIGHTINGS

DATE & TIME:

OBSERVATIONS:

DATE & TIME:

OBSERVATIONS:

DATE & TIME:

OBSERVATIONS:

DATE & TIME:

OBSERVATIONS:

DATE & TIME:

OBSERVATIONS:

BIRD: _____

	DATE & TIME	LOCATION
○ MALE ○ FEMALE		

	STYLE OF FEEDER	FOOD IN FEEDER
VISITED A FEEDER? ○ YES ○ NO		

	TYPE OF WATER SOURCE	
VISITED A WATER SOURCE? ○ YES ○ NO		

ACTIVITIES, BEHAVIORS, AND OTHER OBSERVATIONS

_____
_____
_____
_____
_____
_____
_____
_____
_____
_____
_____
_____

ADDITIONAL SIGHTINGS

DATE & TIME:

OBSERVATIONS:

DATE & TIME:

OBSERVATIONS:

DATE & TIME:

OBSERVATIONS:

DATE & TIME:

OBSERVATIONS:

DATE & TIME:

OBSERVATIONS:

BIRD: _____

	DATE & TIME	LOCATION
○ MALE ○ FEMALE		
VISITED A FEEDER? ○ YES ○ NO ·	STYLE OF FEEDER	FOOD IN FEEDER
VISITED A WATER SOURCE? ○ YES ○ NO	TYPE OF WATER SOURCE	

ACTIVITIES, BEHAVIORS, AND OTHER OBSERVATIONS

_____

_____

_____

_____

_____

_____

_____

_____

_____

_____

_____

_____

_____

ADDITIONAL SIGHTINGS

DATE & TIME:

OBSERVATIONS:

DATE & TIME:

OBSERVATIONS:

DATE & TIME:

OBSERVATIONS:

DATE & TIME:

OBSERVATIONS:

DATE & TIME:

OBSERVATIONS:

BIRD: _____

○ MALE
○ FEMALE

DATE & TIME	LOCATION

	STYLE OF FEEDER	FOOD IN FEEDER
VISITED A FEEDER? ○ YES ○ NO		

	TYPE OF WATER SOURCE
VISITED A WATER SOURCE? ○ YES ○ NO	

ACTIVITIES, BEHAVIORS, AND OTHER OBSERVATIONS

_____

_____

_____

_____

_____

_____

_____

_____

_____

_____

_____

ADDITIONAL SIGHTINGS

DATE & TIME:

OBSERVATIONS:

DATE & TIME:

OBSERVATIONS:

DATE & TIME:

OBSERVATIONS:

DATE & TIME:

OBSERVATIONS:

DATE & TIME:

OBSERVATIONS:

BIRD: _____

	DATE & TIME	LOCATION
○ MALE ○ FEMALE		

	STYLE OF FEEDER	FOOD IN FEEDER
VISITED A FEEDER? ○ YES ○ NO		

	TYPE OF WATER SOURCE
VISITED A WATER SOURCE? ○ YES ○ NO	

ACTIVITIES, BEHAVIORS, AND OTHER OBSERVATIONS

_____

_____

_____

_____

_____

_____

_____

_____

_____

_____

_____

_____

ADDITIONAL SIGHTINGS

DATE & TIME:

OBSERVATIONS:

DATE & TIME:

OBSERVATIONS:

DATE & TIME:

OBSERVATIONS:

DATE & TIME:

OBSERVATIONS:

DATE & TIME:

OBSERVATIONS:

BIRD: _____

○ MALE

○ FEMALE

DATE & TIME	LOCATION

VISITED A FEEDER? ○ YES ○ NO	STYLE OF FEEDER	FOOD IN FEEDER

VISITED A WATER SOURCE? ○ YES ○ NO	TYPE OF WATER SOURCE

ACTIVITIES, BEHAVIORS, AND OTHER OBSERVATIONS

_____

_____

_____

_____

_____

_____

_____

_____

_____

_____

_____

ADDITIONAL SIGHTINGS

DATE & TIME:

OBSERVATIONS:

DATE & TIME:

OBSERVATIONS:

DATE & TIME:

OBSERVATIONS:

DATE & TIME:

OBSERVATIONS:

DATE & TIME:

OBSERVATIONS:

BIRD: _____

	DATE & TIME	LOCATION
○ MALE ○ FEMALE		

	STYLE OF FEEDER	FOOD IN FEEDER
VISITED A FEEDER? ○ YES ○ NO		

	TYPE OF WATER SOURCE	
VISITED A WATER SOURCE? ○ YES ○ NO		

ACTIVITIES, BEHAVIORS, AND OTHER OBSERVATIONS

_____
_____
_____
_____
_____
_____
_____
_____
_____
_____
_____
_____

ADDITIONAL SIGHTINGS

DATE & TIME:

OBSERVATIONS:

DATE & TIME:

OBSERVATIONS:

DATE & TIME:

OBSERVATIONS:

DATE & TIME:

OBSERVATIONS:

DATE & TIME:

OBSERVATIONS:

BIRD: _____

	DATE & TIME	LOCATION
○ MALE ○ FEMALE		

VISITED A FEEDER? ○ YES ○ NO	STYLE OF FEEDER	FOOD IN FEEDER

VISITED A WATER SOURCE? ○ YES ○ NO	TYPE OF WATER SOURCE	

ACTIVITIES, BEHAVIORS, AND OTHER OBSERVATIONS

_____

_____

_____

_____

_____

_____

_____

_____

_____

_____

_____

_____

ADDITIONAL SIGHTINGS

DATE & TIME:

OBSERVATIONS:

DATE & TIME:

OBSERVATIONS:

DATE & TIME:

OBSERVATIONS:

DATE & TIME:

OBSERVATIONS:

DATE & TIME:

OBSERVATIONS:

BIRD: _____

○ MALE

○ FEMALE

DATE & TIME	LOCATION

	STYLE OF FEEDER	FOOD IN FEEDER
VISITED A FEEDER? ○ YES ○ NO		

	TYPE OF WATER SOURCE	
VISITED A WATER SOURCE? ○ YES ○ NO		

ACTIVITIES, BEHAVIORS, AND OTHER OBSERVATIONS

_____

_____

_____

_____

_____

_____

_____

_____

_____

_____

_____

_____

ADDITIONAL SIGHTINGS

DATE & TIME:

OBSERVATIONS:

DATE & TIME:

OBSERVATIONS:

DATE & TIME:

OBSERVATIONS:

DATE & TIME:

OBSERVATIONS:

DATE & TIME:

OBSERVATIONS:

BIRD: _____

	DATE & TIME	LOCATION
○ MALE ○ FEMALE		

	STYLE OF FEEDER	FOOD IN FEEDER
VISITED A FEEDER? ○ YES ○ NO		

	TYPE OF WATER SOURCE	
VISITED A WATER SOURCE? ○ YES ○ NO		

ACTIVITIES, BEHAVIORS, AND OTHER OBSERVATIONS

_____

_____

_____

_____

_____

_____

_____

_____

_____

_____

_____

_____

ADDITIONAL SIGHTINGS

DATE & TIME:

OBSERVATIONS:

DATE & TIME:

OBSERVATIONS:

DATE & TIME:

OBSERVATIONS:

DATE & TIME:

OBSERVATIONS:

DATE & TIME:

OBSERVATIONS:

BIRD: _____

	DATE & TIME	LOCATION
○ MALE ○ FEMALE		

	STYLE OF FEEDER	FOOD IN FEEDER
VISITED A FEEDER? ○ YES ○ NO		

	TYPE OF WATER SOURCE
VISITED A WATER SOURCE? ○ YES ○ NO	

ACTIVITIES, BEHAVIORS, AND OTHER OBSERVATIONS

_____

_____

_____

_____

_____

_____

_____

_____

_____

_____

_____

_____

ADDITIONAL SIGHTINGS

DATE & TIME:

OBSERVATIONS:

DATE & TIME:

OBSERVATIONS:

DATE & TIME:

OBSERVATIONS:

DATE & TIME:

OBSERVATIONS:

DATE & TIME:

OBSERVATIONS:

BIRD: _____

	DATE & TIME	LOCATION
◯ MALE		
◯ FEMALE		

	STYLE OF FEEDER	FOOD IN FEEDER
VISITED A FEEDER? ◯ YES ◯ NO		

	TYPE OF WATER SOURCE
VISITED A WATER SOURCE? ◯ YES ◯ NO	

ACTIVITIES, BEHAVIORS, AND OTHER OBSERVATIONS

_____

_____

_____

_____

_____

_____

_____

_____

_____

_____

_____

_____

_____

ADDITIONAL SIGHTINGS

DATE & TIME:

OBSERVATIONS:

DATE & TIME:

OBSERVATIONS:

DATE & TIME:

OBSERVATIONS:

DATE & TIME:

OBSERVATIONS:

DATE & TIME:

OBSERVATIONS:

BIRD: _____

○ MALE
○ FEMALE

DATE & TIME	LOCATION

	STYLE OF FEEDER	FOOD IN FEEDER
VISITED A FEEDER? ○ YES ○ NO		

	TYPE OF WATER SOURCE
VISITED A WATER SOURCE? ○ YES ○ NO	

ACTIVITIES, BEHAVIORS, AND OTHER OBSERVATIONS

_____

_____

_____

_____

_____

_____

_____

_____

_____

_____

_____

_____

ADDITIONAL SIGHTINGS

DATE & TIME:

OBSERVATIONS:

DATE & TIME:

OBSERVATIONS:

DATE & TIME:

OBSERVATIONS:

DATE & TIME:

OBSERVATIONS:

DATE & TIME:

OBSERVATIONS:

BIRD: _____

	DATE & TIME	LOCATION
○ MALE ○ FEMALE		

VISITED A FEEDER? ○ YES ○ NO	STYLE OF FEEDER	FOOD IN FEEDER

VISITED A WATER SOURCE? ○ YES ○ NO	TYPE OF WATER SOURCE	

ACTIVITIES, BEHAVIORS, AND OTHER OBSERVATIONS

_____

_____

_____

_____

_____

_____

_____

_____

_____

_____

_____

_____

ADDITIONAL SIGHTINGS

DATE & TIME:

OBSERVATIONS:

DATE & TIME:

OBSERVATIONS:

DATE & TIME:

OBSERVATIONS:

DATE & TIME:

OBSERVATIONS:

DATE & TIME:

OBSERVATIONS:

BIRD: _____

	DATE & TIME	LOCATION
○ MALE ○ FEMALE		

	STYLE OF FEEDER	FOOD IN FEEDER
VISITED A FEEDER? ○ YES ○ NO		

	TYPE OF WATER SOURCE
VISITED A WATER SOURCE? ○ YES ○ NO	

ACTIVITIES, BEHAVIORS, AND OTHER OBSERVATIONS

_____

_____

_____

_____

_____

_____

_____

_____

_____

_____

_____

_____

ADDITIONAL SIGHTINGS

DATE & TIME:

OBSERVATIONS:

DATE & TIME:

OBSERVATIONS:

DATE & TIME:

OBSERVATIONS:

DATE & TIME:

OBSERVATIONS:

DATE & TIME:

OBSERVATIONS:

ADDITIONAL SIGHTINGS

DATE & TIME:

OBSERVATIONS:

DATE & TIME:

OBSERVATIONS:

DATE & TIME:

OBSERVATIONS:

DATE & TIME:

OBSERVATIONS:

DATE & TIME:

OBSERVATIONS:

Most Common Backyard Birds

- ⭕ American Crow
- ⭕ American Goldfinch
- ⭕ American Robin
- ⭕ American Tree Sparrow
- ⭕ Baltimore Oriole
- ⭕ Bewick's Wren
- ⭕ Black-capped Chickadee
- ⭕ Black-chinned Hummingbird
- ⭕ Blue Jay
- ⭕ Brown-headed Cowbird
- ⭕ Brown Thrasher
- ⭕ Bushtit
- ⭕ Carolina Wren
- ⭕ Chipping Sparrow
- ⭕ Common Grackle
- ⭕ Dark-eyed Junco
- ⭕ Downy Woodpecker
- ⭕ Eastern Bluebird
- ⭕ Eastern Phoebe
- ⭕ Eurasian Collared-Dove
- ⭕ European Starling
- ⭕ Fox Sparrow
- ⭕ Gray Catbird
- ⭕ Hairy Woodpecker
- ⭕ House Finch

- ⭕ House Sparrow
- ⭕ House Wren
- ⭕ Lesser Goldfinch
- ⭕ Mourning Dove
- ⭕ Northern Cardinal
- ⭕ Northern Flicker
- ⭕ Northern Mockingbird
- ⭕ Pileated Woodpecker
- ⭕ Pine Siskin
- ⭕ Pine Warbler
- ⭕ Purple Finch
- ⭕ Purple Martin
- ⭕ Red-bellied Woodpecker
- ⭕ Red-breasted Nuthatch
- ⭕ Red-winged Blackbird
- ⭕ Rose-breasted Grosbeak
- ⭕ Ruby-throated Hummingbird
- ⭕ Song Sparrow
- ⭕ Spotted Towhee
- ⭕ Tufted Titmouse
- ⭕ Varied Thrush
- ⭕ White-breasted Nuthatch
- ⭕ White-crowned Sparrow
- ⭕ White-throated Sparrow
- ⭕ Yellow-rumped Warbler

ENJOY THE BEAUTY OF WILD BIRDS WHEREVER YOU LIVE!

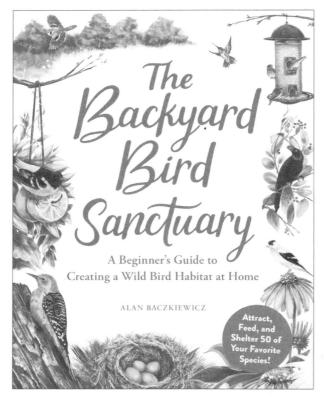

PICK UP OR DOWNLOAD YOUR COPY TODAY!